Habitat Explorer

# Gardens and Parks

## Nick Baker

Collins

For my niece Rowan and the many adventures we are yet to have.

First published in 2006 by
Collins, an imprint of
HarperCollinsPublishers
77-85 Fulham Palace Road
Hammersmith
London W6 8JB

www.collins.co.uk

Collins is a registered trademark of HarperCollins Publishers Ltd

12 11 10 09 08 07 06
7 6 5 4 3 2 1

Editorial director: Helen Brocklehurst
Editor: Emma Callery
Designer: Sue Miller
Photographer: Nikki English, except for those pictures credited below
Flick book illustrations: Lizzie Harper
Editorial assistant: Julia Koppitz
Production: Graham Cook

ISBN 0-00-720766-2
ISBN -13 978-0-00-720766-4

Colour Reproductions by Dot Gradations Ltd, UK
Printed and bound in Hong Kong by Printing Express

Photograph credits (b = bottom, l = left, m = middle, r = right, t = top)
Page 5 (t), 6, 9 (tr, bl, br), 32, 40, 42 (b), 43 (t, m), 45 (t), 48 (t), 49 (m), 50: © Paul Sterry/Nature Photographers Ltd;
8: © Philip Newman/Nature Photographers Ltd; 9 (tl), 36 (t): © Hugh Clark/Nature Photographers Ltd;
15 (r): © Michael Chinery; 16 (t), 51 (t), 67 (t): © Stephen Dalton/NHPA; 22, 23 (tr), 39 (b): © C J Wildbird Foods/David White; 24: © Bill Coster/NHPA; 36 (b): © S C Bisserot; 38: © E A Janes; 42 (t): © Andrew Cleave/Nature Photographers Ltd; 43 (b): © Colin Varndell; 45 (b), 60: © Nicholas Phelps Brown; 49 (bl): © Alan Barnes/NHPA; 51 (l): © Anthony Bannister/NHPA; 51 (m): © Robert Thompson/NHPA; 51 (b): © Laurie Campbell/NHPA; 56: © Science Photo; 57 (t): © Derek Middleton/FLPA; 57 (m): © NHPA; 62 (t): © Geoff du Feu/Nature Photographers Ltd; 62 (b), 63 (m): © N A Callow/Nature Photographers Ltd; 63 (r): © Daniel Heuclin/NHPA.

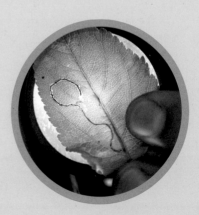

# Contents

Flick the pages to see the bird fly!

# Your local patch

There is no place like home. You may not think of looking for adventure among the patio tubs, behind the woodpile or even in the potting shed or window box, but it is there in abundance. The trick is to change your perspective on life, look at things from a different place and in a new way.

**You may feel there is no interesting wildlife** for hundreds of miles, but change your scale a bit and you can be running with predators every bit as ferocious as a lion or tiger. You can stalk creatures as exotic and alien in their appearance as any bird of paradise and witness phenomena that would boggle the mind of even the most world-weary scientist – all within a few metres of where you are sitting right now!

**You don't believe me?** Get out there and look. This book is about giving you wings to explore this seemingly familiar environment. Within these pages I give away little tips and tricks that make the natural world reveal itself in amazing ways. The pages are peppered with suggestions of things to look out for and – of course – some of the easier ways to interact with wildlife and make your own patch more attractive to the small creatures that live in your garden, window box or patio.

**The basic requirements of life** include somewhere to live and preferably with the other essentials to fuel and nourish: namely food and water. Even if you live somewhere that seems like a concrete desert, get down and look into the cracks and crevices and here you will find all the essentials for life. You just might be surprised as to what is living close to your own home. Look at a crack in a patio; this is shelter for something very small as, in here, there will be moisture and warmth.

**You can also create homes and provide food and water** to boost the number of species sharing your space; these ideas and more are explored within the pages of this book. Remember, though, this is not a comprehensive guide, so have fun, experiment and think about other ways you can encourage and study the wildlife around you.

Home Sweet Home – you may be lucky enough to have swallows nesting under your eaves.

All flowers lure insects; from bees and hoverflies to butterflies, they all add interest to your garden.

Where you have flying insects, you will also start attracting those that feed on them – birds, bats and, of course, spiders.

# Handy stuff for exploring with

 **What kit you will need to explore your garden or park** with very much depends on what your patch is like. If you have a little back yard in the city with hardly enough space to swing a net, you will explore it differently to someone who has a mountain in theirs. Having said this, there is interest to be found in any garden from an estate to a window box, and so here are a few bits of kit that I would find useful when exploring.

**Binoculars** These are always very useful, especially if you want to watch the details of the lives of birds and other insects without disturbing them. A pair of binoculars may be quite expensive to buy, but they are invaluable to a serious naturalist.

**Magnifying glass/pocket microscope** Most things you can make or improvise with, but a hand lens is an essential bit of kit. It needn't be expensive and you can pick one up for pocket money. If you want to turn greenfly into monsters, though, you may need a pocket microscope. This is a bit more expensive, but worth every penny and still a fraction of the price of a Playstation!

**Notebook and pen/pencil** Another one of those naturalist's staples, it's always good to make notes, keep diaries and draw the things you notice. It is something all the great naturalists from Darwin to Bill Oddie have done. It is surprising just how much and quickly we forget details.

**Plastic pots and jars** These are a staple of any naturalist anywhere; handy for storing specimens, rearing insects or simply holding onto something while you inspect it with a magnifying glass. Plastic bags can do a similar job and you can keep a handful in your pocket at any time. They are useful for storing botanical plants and, if you blow them up and tie the tops with string, you can make temporary containers from them.

**Sieves** You may be surprised, but meshed scooping devices from sieves to tea strainers can make very handy little catching devices! They can be used like a net in water or modified into a pair of bug-catching tongs. Use larger sieves to sift through soil to find small creatures and moth pupae.

**Trowel** I find this handy for investigating the soil, exhuming worms and, of course, for re-digging any footprints you might leave on your parents' flower beds. It's always a good idea not to upset those garden proud grown-ups.

Plastic boxes

Glass jar

Microscope

Test tubes

Small sieve

Magnifying glass

Magnifying lens

Notebook and pen

Plastic bags

Binoculars

Trowel

## Take my advice

* Because this book is about attracting things to your garden and providing homes and feeding stations, there is obviously plenty of creating to be done. This means there are sections and activities that involve hammers, nails, screws and even the odd drill and other power tools. These things can be a little tricky to use and can be dangerous.

* So before you start any of the projects, let a grown-up know what you are up to and, if you are using specialist tools, ask for help.

# Our feathered friends

Birds are everywhere, and because they are big, they are often the first creatures to catch our attention. They also show us how we can provide for nature in our own back yards. In fact, if it wasn't for our feathered friends, we wouldn't be seeing our gardens and parks as wildlife refuges at all. Birds invented wildlife-friendly gardening!

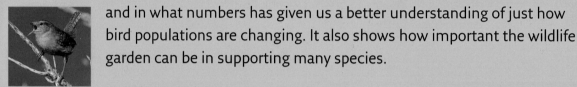

**In recent years, watching birds in gardens** and being aware of who visits and in what numbers has given us a better understanding of just how bird populations are changing. It also shows how important the wildlife garden can be in supporting many species.

**There are many products, catalogues and shops** dedicated to encouraging birds into your garden, and once you have gained their interest, the feeling of successfully helping them makes your heart glow. So why stop at birds, why not encourage butterflies and other insects, mammals and reptiles, and amphibians, too?

**There is more to encouraging birds into your garden** than hanging out a bag of nuts or throwing out some crumbs or stale bacon rind when the generous mood takes you! Birds are feathered ambassadors for what we humans can do for wildlife. Just by nailing together a few planks of wood and providing a variety of food and a source of water, we can make their lives easier. They will return the favour by giving us a little glimpse into their often fascinating lives.

**Bird populations in the wild depend mainly on two things:** first they need food, and second they need somewhere to live and nest. So if you are to make your local patch of interest to our feathered friends you need to bear these things in mind.

A house sparrow: these chirpy little birds are associated with our homes and buildings but, for some reason, their numbers are declining in their natural range in Europe. Here is a bird we can help by feeding them and providing nest sites.

Swallows love to nest on our homes and outhouses. It's hard to imagine that they come all the way from central and southern Africa every summer just to stick mud together under our eaves!

The European starling is a noisy city dweller that gathers in impressively huge flocks in the winter.

The wren is the king of the singers; a small bird with a loud voice that loves a garden with untidy corners and dense shrubs.

# It's a two-way relationship

**Feeding the birds** is probably the single most popular way in which people interact with the natural world; from feeding pigeons on the park bench to the bird table in the garden. What you are doing is simply taking on the needs and requirements of the birds.

**The ways you can present food to birds** is becoming very big business, and by using the right mix and the right feeder in the right place, you can attract birds almost to order! But for now, here's a low-budget idea to get you going (see opposite).

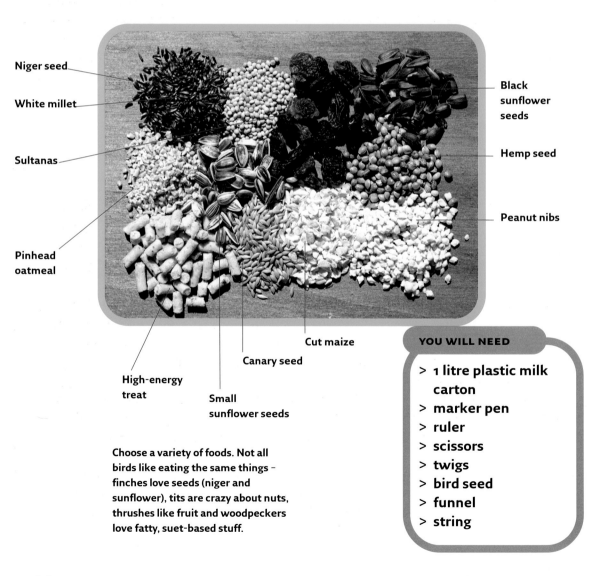

Niger seed

White millet

Sultanas

Pinhead oatmeal

High-energy treat

Small sunflower seeds

Canary seed

Cut maize

Black sunflower seeds

Hemp seed

Peanut nibs

Choose a variety of foods. Not all birds like eating the same things – finches love seeds (niger and sunflower), tits are crazy about nuts, thrushes like fruit and woodpeckers love fatty, suet-based stuff.

## YOU WILL NEED

> **1 litre plastic milk carton**
> **marker pen**
> **ruler**
> **scissors**
> **twigs**
> **bird seed**
> **funnel**
> **string**

**1** Using the marker pen and ruler, draw a line 1.5cm from the bottom of the plastic milk carton and parallel to the base on the opposite side to the handle.

**2** With the scissors, cut along the marked line and then, at each end of the incision, cut up about 3cm.

**3** Fold the flap you have just created back into the bottle and add a perch or two. Make these from twigs or any straight bits of wood; push them into a hole below the feeding tray.

**4** Fill with seeds, pouring them into the container through a funnel. Screw the lid back on and then hang up the container with string in your garden.

## Take my advice

* Position your feeders carefully. Birds like to be in the open so that predators cannot sneak up on them. But they also like to have cover nearby so that if a sparrow hawk comes cruising around, they can all leap into cover.

* Vary the locations of your feeders, as some birds are bold while others are shy. So feed close to the house by all means, but do not forget the nervous ones and provide food at the end of the garden too.

* Different birds feed in different ways. Some rarely get onto the bird table but prefer to stay on the ground, while others like flat surfaces, and some like to hang.

* Feed only good quality foods. If it's cheap, it may have lots of wheat in it. Cheaper peanuts may also contain a fungus infection that can kill the birds you are helping.

# Nutty feeders

**The cheapest nut feeder has to be a plastic mesh bag,** the sort that supermarket fruit often comes in. Simply stuff it with peanuts and hang it up. I hate the bright orange of the netting but I have noticed that siskins (one of my favourite birds) show the most interest in these feeders even though they have many others (some of them scarily expensive too) to choose from. This could well become a subject for a garden experiment!

**Alternatively, make a full-fat nut pudding.** This animal fat-based food is made from warmed animal fat or suet, mixed with any variety of seeds, fruits, nuts or insects and left to set before being served up. It's a great way of providing a high-energy winter diet for your birds. My favourite way to use the suet reciped is to make fat cones – see opposite – or dip teasel heads into the melted suet.

**Another way to provide bird cake** is to leave the mix to set in a tin that is wedged in place between three blocks screwed to your bird table. Or you can form a ball and stuff it in a handy plastic fruit net; fill an old coconut shell; or drill holes in a log and jam the fat into these. This last is a real favourite for woodpeckers! This recipe is very easy to make and you can fine tune the ingredients, perhaps including some peanuts, sunflower seeds or millet, according to what the birds seem to prefer.

## Take my advice

* If you have just started feeding the birds in your garden, it may take them a little while to learn about your new service. So be patient and if after a few weeks there are still no visitors, try relocating your feeding station. It may be that the birds feel just a little too exposed.

* Keep your feeders clean by washing and sterilizing them every few months and try to avoid food hanging around and becoming stale. Feeders over concrete or decking mean you can easily sweep away any spilled food, which may otherwise attract unwanted wildlife such as rats.

**1** Next time you are out for a walk collect old dry pine cones in various sizes. When you get home, tie some string around the base of a few of them.

**2** Take a saucepan and heat the suet slowly in it until it has melted. Add the peanut butter and mix in until it has melted too.

**3** Add some flour to help thicken the mixture and then pour in plenty of small fine seeds until you have a fairly stiff mixture. Let it cool a little, continuing to stir.

**4** Before the mixture sets, drop your cones into the pan and press the stodge in between the scales.

**5** Leave to cool and harden and then take out to the garden to hang in a tree or on a bird table.

# A bird in the hand ...

**If being close to wildlife** is your goal, then it doesn't get much closer than when it is sitting on your palm. The robin is the perfect candidate for this. Famously bold, you can train your local bird to come to your hand in as little as a week – see opposite for how you do it. If at any stage you fail, go back a step and keep trying for contact. It is worth it for both of you: your robin will get vital food of the right kind, and you will get the rare thrill of touching a wild bird.

## Take my advice

* Despite what some people seem to think, you can feed your birds all year round, just be aware that large, dry food items, such as stale bread crusts and peanuts, can choke young nestlings. So in the summer, either place them in a feeder that allows the birds to only take small bits or crumble and crush the food first.

* Also, don't panic if you have to go away and your feeders run out. The birds are used to having food resources in the wild that do the same thing. They are adaptable and will find food elsewhere until you resume feeding again.

**1** Get your robin interested by catching its eye with a plastic container full of wriggling meal worms. Start by simply placing this tub on your regular bird table. Eventually the robin will start feeding on them.

**4** Then, when he seems quite relaxed, one day remove the tub and place the wrigglers in your palm. You should now have a hand tame robin!

**3** ... then move it into the middle of the lawn. Try standing out in the garden while he is feeding, progressively getting closer to him – a step or two every day. Now you can try offering the meal worm in the same tub but at arm's length.

**2** Then slowly, as the days go by, move the meal worm container away from the bird table. First move it to the foot of the bird table ...

## Nick's trick

Different robins have different tolerance levels so there are no rules to how long getting to within arm's length will take. Just be patient. Keeping low or even lying down all help.

## Take it further

Meal worms are the wriggly larvae of various beetles and can be bought in many pet shops, especially those that deal with reptiles and amphibians. They are really easy to culture in a box in your airing cupboard. All you need is a well-ventilated box with a tight-fitting lid; you can feed the worms on oatmeal, bread, biscuits and the like. Feeding meal worms to the birds is a little trickier, though, as the worms thoughtlessly have a tendency to crawl off, something a peanut most definitely cannot do. Overcome this by serving them up in slippery sided containers – but watch out for rain.

# Making a simple bird table

**Go to any garden centre and take a look at the bird tables that are available.** You can get them with balconies, balustrades, porches, even thatched roofs and chimneys. Some even come with a nest box upstairs! Personally, I think that some of them are just too ornate and in my experience, although they can all work to a greater or lesser degree, they fall short of actually providing what the birds want and need, which is a nice stable, spacious platform that is easy to keep clean.

**Bird will eat off pretty much anything** and, as with all things to do with wildlife, there are no hard and fast rules, so you can experiment. To get you started, here is a very simple and effective step-by-step project to build a bird table.

**1** The piece of plywood is the feeding platform and to this you need to attach the edging strips, two of which are a little shorter than the shorter sides of the plywood to give you gaps in the corners for making it easier to sweep clean. They also allow rainwater to drain off.

**2** Screw the edging strips to the board. Use at least two screws on each short strip and three on the longer edges. At this stage, you can paint and protect the bird table with a water-based preservative, which will stop the wood rotting.

**3** Now attach your table to the post using the angle brackets, screwing the brackets to the post first.

**4** Screw the brackets to the bottom of the feeding platform. You could also attach some hooks to the post and to the corners on the underside of the table to hang seed feeders and bird cakes from. Choose the location for your bird table and drive your post into the ground as far as it will go, with a minimum of 40cm under the ground's surface. You can now coat this with wood preservative too.

### YOU WILL NEED

> 35 x 50cm piece of marine or exterior quality plywood, a minimum of 1cm thick
> 130 x 1 x 1cm batten cut into two 25cm lengths and two 40cm lengths
> 2cm galvanized wood screws
> Phillips screwdriver
> Water-based wood preservative and paintbrush (optional)
> 4 cup hooks
> 1.8m wooden post with a flat top and a sharp end
> 4 angle brackets

# Make a deluxe bird bath

**It's good to provide water for your birds near the feeders.** Let's face it, would you want to eat buckets full of cereal or crisps without a drink to wash it all down? Birds will not only want to drink regularly but they also need to wash and keep their feathers clean.

**The best way of providing water is an old tray, dish or dustbin lid** filled with water. Pop a rock or a branch in it so your visitors have somewhere to perch too. In the winter it is even more vital to provide water, but you must make sure the water doesn't freeze over. Break up any ice that forms as soon as possible. Alternatively, make this handsome bird bath with just a few ingredients.

When you first turn over your bird bath there may be bits of cabbage stuck in it. Either cut them out with scissors or let nature take its course and they will soon shrivel up and die.

## YOU WILL NEED

> a board
> 5kg bag grit sand
> big cabbage
> 5kg bag ready-mix cement
> water
> an old bucket
> stick
> rubber gloves
> polythene sheet (or plastic bag)

**1** First tip out the sand onto the board and make a mound out of it. The mound represents the depth and the size of your bird bath, so use your imagination.

**2** Now cut the leaves off your cabbage, keeping them whole. Place them over the sand mound with their stems meeting in the middle.

**3** Empty the bag of cement into the bucket and add water according to the instructions on the bag. Stir it thoroughly with a strong stick.

**4** Pour the cement mix onto the top of the cabbage leaves and then, wearing the rubber gloves, spread it over the mound to a depth of at least 3cm.

**5** Make sure the cabbage leaves, and any sand that is showing through the leaves, are well covered with the cement. Then smooth the top of the cement to a round or flat shape, depending on what you're going to stand the bird bath on when it's finished.

**6** Cover the whole thing with polythene and leave to dry for at least a day. When the cement is dry, turn over the bath, remove the board, scoop out the sand, remove the leaves and you have it – a designer, custom-made bird bath with a beautiful, yet non-slip, leafy design in the bottom of it. You can varnish or paint it if you wish and then keep it filled with fresh clean water for happy splashy birds.

# Make a nest box

**Birds are experiencing a housing crisis** and the reason there are not enough nest sites is – you've guessed it – us humans. We have a tendency to tidy up the countryside and our gardens too much. All too often, dead trees that offer all sorts of habitats, crevices and holes are seen as a public safety hazard and so are cut down, just to be on the safe side. Even healthy trees are axed because a knot hole may get infected and kill the tree.

**As a result of our human paranoia,** the traditional nesting site for many of our small woodland birds – the hole – is sadly becoming a rare thing. So here is yet another way we can provide for our birds and at the same time learn an awful lot about their private lives; it comes in the form of a tit box.

**This classic design – a wooden box with a hole in it** – is the basis of many other boxes that cater for the needs and requirements of other species. Here I show you how to make the basic design, and if you get adventurous, overleaf are a few simple modifications and other ideas.

**Making this nest box does require a little bit of woodwork.** Now, I am useless with my hands but even I can make a half decent tit box that no self-respecting tit would turn its beak up at. So give it a go. Let's face it, a bird box is one woodwork lesson with an end product that will not be gathering dust on top of the wardrobe.

## Cutting plan for your wood

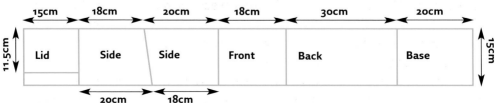

## YOU WILL NEED

> **a plank of untreated wood that is 15cm wide, 1.5cm thick and 121cm long**
> **saw**
> **electric drill with plug cutter and wood drill bits**
> **2.5cm galvanized wood screws**
> **Phillips screwdriver**
> **2 hinges**

**1** Ask an adult to help you cut up the wood as shown in the plan opposite. Use a special 5cm plug cutter fitting on the electric drill to make the hole in the front. With a wooden drill bit, also make holes in the base for drainage. Then lay out the pieces as shown in this picture.

**2** Using the Phillips screwdriver, screw the sides to the base, at the top and bottom.

**3** Screw the front to the sides and base. Again, use a screw at the top and bottom of each edge. Do the same with the back, ensuring the extra length is sticking out the top of the box, rather than the bottom.

**4** The only piece you do not nail down is the lid; this is how you will access the nest box in the winter to clean it out once a year, so attach two hinges at one side of the lid.

**5** Fasten the hinges to the back of the box ensuring a snug fit. There – it really is that simple. Once you have got the hang of it you could make several for around your garden. They also make great presents and you can put surprise gifts in them as well. For hanging details, see the following two pages.

# Positioning your nest box

**You have your nest box, now where do you nail it?** Well it does depend a little on the species that you want to attract. But you have to get several factors right. Height is the first one, it needs to be high enough for the birds to feel secure – 3m is a good height for most common garden birds. Shelter is also very important as no bird wants cold rain driving in their front door, so somewhere protected from the elements, the cold, wet and sun is a good idea.

**But on top of all this you have to balance the birds' requirements** with 'viewability' because it is always interesting to see the comings and goings of your residents. Experiment by putting up boxes in different locations and at different heights. Then be patient – some boxes to not seem suitable until they have weathered a season or two first. If you are still not having much luck, try another spot.

**Positioning your nest is a compromise between the needs of the birds and the needs of the naturalist, who will want to keep an eye on things.**

## Take it further

* Now you have got the hang of making a bird box, you could try varying the size of the entrance holes to try to attract some different birds.
> 29mm: tits and tits only
> 32mm: good for your chunky sparrows
> 45mm: starlings
> Cut the front in half: robins, flycatchers, blackbirds.

* You will also do better with sparrows if you get lots of nest boxes and put them all close together to create a sparrow terrace.

* If you have a wooded and wild garden, you could try making owl or kestrel boxes, or even a special one for treecreepers; but this is getting a little specialized so on page 71 there is more information.

Here is a classic wooden design of bird box, much tried and tested by birds and people, next to the latest thing in bird residencies: woodcrete. This strong mix of wood and concrete may be more expensive but it should last a lot longer than wood alone. Predators also find it hard to nibble and chisel through.

Spotted flycatcher/ robin/ thrush

Woodcrete tit box

Little owl

Roosting pocket for wrens

House sparrow terrace

House martin

Barn owl

Swallow

Kestrel

Blue tit

Convertible box for open front and hole nester

# Make a rain guage

**By catching and storing rainwater,** you are helping to make the most of a valuable resource. You might want to put a water butt in your garden so that you can store larger quantities. About 100,000 litres of rain falls on the roof of your house each year, so if you connect it to the guttering from your roof, you will be able to collect a large amount.

**Rainwater has far more nutrients and doesn't have the lime found in tap water,** nor has it been treated with the chemicals that drinking water has, so it's better for a lot of creatures and plants. In fact, algae love rainwater so much that you will probably find your rainwater supply gets green and slimy pretty quickly.

**To make the rain gauge opposite** you will need to ask an adult to cut the bottom off an old plastic drinks bottle and between you twist garden wire around it to make a support that can then be hung on a fence or other suitable place. Then follow the steps opposite for how to use your rain gauge.

**Make sure there isn't anything sticking out over the top** of the place you choose to hang your rain gauge. You must be able to catch the maximum amount of rain possible.

## Fab fact

By the time your supply of rainwater is a few days old there will be hundreds of microscopic creatures living in it. In fact, the first microscope was invented in 1675 by a Dutch merchant called Anton van Leeuwenhoek, who discovered lots of living creatures in a pot of rainwater that had stood outside his house for a few days.

**1** Tie a piece of string around the pillar or perhaps a treen trunk from which you will hang your gauge. If you are using a fence, bang in a nail.

**2** Insert the metal loop at the top of the wire frame into the string support. Go away and wait for the rain to fall.

**3** Either mark on the container the level of each day's rainfall – it might be easier to take the container out of the frame to do this – or ...

**4** ... measure the amount of rainfall with a ruler and make a note of it – see also 'Take it further' to the right.

## Take it further

* Keep a log book of weekly or monthly rainfall.

* If you keep it going for a few years, you'll be able to see how the rainfall differs from year to year.

* You can also use a jar to see how much water is in snow. Put an inch of snow in a jar, then bring it inside and let it melt. Heavy wet snow will have a lot more water in it than dry fluffy snow.

# Fluff and stuff for nest building

**Even before the spring gets going properly,** garden birds are already starting to rummage around securing nest sites and building for the approaching new nesting season. It is at this time of the year that birds have other needs. They have to build nests to insulate their brood and stop their eggs from rolling about, and for that they need building materials.

**You can turn your garden into a bird builders' merchant** and at the same time have a little fun, not only by watching the birds trying to transport the stuff to the nest, but also by watching which species use what materials. The rules are similar to feeding the birds, try offering a variety of materials in different ways. To make a nest bag, see the steps opposite.

## YOU WILL NEED

> **old sock or stocking**
> **mixture of nesting materials (see Step 1)**
> **string**
> **scissors**

**1** This is a great way of using mum's old tights or even that odd sock that seems to have lost its partner in the wash. Collect a variety of materials, such as dried grass, straw, hay, feathers and wool. Add some animal hair and wool collected from barbed wire fences or from your dog or cat's grooming brush, and even from your hair brush! All these things make excellent materials for different birds to weave into nests.

**2** Spread out your collection on some plates so you can take your pick of which items you will stuff into the sock or tights. Look at an old nest in the winter and you will see some are lined with mud and moss and finished with a warm, fluffy layer of fine grass, wool, hair and feathers designed to keep the eggs and the chicks cosy.

**3** Start stuffing your stocking or sock, making sure you get a good mixture of the materials, pushing them right down to the foot.

**4** Separate the different materials by either twisting and knotting the stocking or tying off portions of the sock with string.

**5** Cut little holes in the sock and pull some of the stuffing through to allow the birds to see what's on offer. Go and hang the sock somewhere where you can see it and watch and wait.

## Take it further

* Because most nests are built of different kinds of material and many birds have their own favourites, you may need to provide other stuff, too. As well as using the sock method, you can put on a builder's buffet.

* Collect a selection of shallow bowls and trays and in each put a different building material; try a big tray of wet mud and you might get house martins and swallows coming down to collect it. Blackbirds, thrushes and even potter wasps may also visit the buffet table.

* Moss is also used by many species and coarser straw, and fine sticks and twigs may be taken away by everything from chaffinches to crows.

# Homes and holes

This chapter is all about providing a comfortable home for your wildlife and the great thing is that it doesn't matter if you have a window box or a postage stamp for a garden, you can still create a habitat or two, even if it is just a small one. Little habitats are homes to little things and lots of little habitats make up one bigger one!

**Providing food is a way of attracting wildlife** to your garden and once you have achieved that, the challenge is to get your visitors to stay. There is a huge range of products out there on the market – homes and houses for everything from ladybirds and toads to bees and badgers – and even though there are plenty of addresses on pages 70–1 for various stockists, many of the basics can be made at home very cheaply. Sometimes it doesn't even require much creativity. A nettle patch or an area of long grass, for example, may look untidy to you, but it will provide more homes and hideouts for wildlife than you might at first imagine.

**The lawn can look like a great big green desert** spread out in front of your house. No good but to play football on, right? Well, us humans have a habit of raking and tidying up this carpet of grass, but it can provide a home for that king of wigglers, the intestines of the soil – the worms. They are not only good for the garden soil – turning it, aerating it and fertilizing it – they will also provide indirectly much food for many other mammals and birds. In turn, this provides entertainment for us naturalists.

**The other garden desert, concrete,** is also hard to imagine as being much of a habitat, but inevitably it cracks and in these yawning canyons a colony of ants can fit. The concrete works as a giant storage heater, giving protection from the elements and providing the ideal base for these gardeners' friends to base their exploits.

Wild grass attracts insects and small mammals.

Worm heaven.

Small holes will attract many an insect such as wasps and beetles.

Between each paving stone lurk thousands of ants.

A bat box is a larger home that you can make yourself.

# Make a bumblebee box

**We all love bumblebees.** Maybe it's because they look cuddly and pollinate our flowers and fruit trees, or perhaps they simply remind us of happy times as they are the first of the insects in the spring to brave the chilly weather. They are able to do this because they have a special way of dislocating their wings and revving their big flight muscles to generate body heat (a bit like our shivering).

**You can make your garden a haven for these fluffy little fellas** by creating some nest sites for them. In the wild, they usually use the old burrows of mice or similar dark, dry crevices. This is what the queens are doing when they first emerge in the spring and you can watch them searching any dark hole. This is the time of year you need to get your box out if you are to stand any chance of a queen moving in.

**If you are providing nest boxes for bees, why not provide them with food too – in the form of nectar-rich flowers.**

## Take my advice

* Bees can be fickle and fussy so to increase your chances, make a few nests and try them in different positions.

* Keep an eye on your nests for coming and going bee action. This will tell you that you have a colony starting up.

* Make your garden super bee friendly by planting a variety of nectar-rich flowers.

**1** There is not much making required here; all you need to do is choose a sunny location – south facing is ideal – and dig a hole deep enough and the right shape to take your chosen pot upside down. This doesn't have to be on level ground, it could be in a bank.

**2** Take the chicken wire and put a big fist full of nesting material in the centre of it.

**3** Scrunch up the chicken wire – be very careful of any sharp pieces that might be sticking out the side – so that the bedding material is safely enclosed. Push the bundle into the flower pot.

**4** Turn the flower pot upside down and put into your freshly dug hole. Push the hose pipe into the central drainage hole in the bottom – now the top! – of the flower pot. This will become the entrance for the bees.

**5** Cover any extra holes with stones and return the soil around and over the pot. Surround the entrance with stones or logs to give the bees some privacy and wait for a questing queen to stick her head in.

# The 'embryo' nest

**Just the sight of a wasp's yellow-and-black striped uniform** sends many of us into an arm-flapping panic. Social wasps – or yellow jackets as they are called in America – are much feared, mainly because they have the ability to get our attention by using their sharp and venom-loaded sting. But get past this and you will be surprised by what you will find.

**They are actually one of my favourite creatures;** colourful, interesting, great pollinators of flowers and fruit trees and, of course, something that gets overlooked. They are, in fact, brilliant and efficient predators of many garden pests such as caterpillars and aphids. It's a shame that the sting gets in the way.

**If you want to witness the beauty of a wasps' nest** without the threatening presence of thousands of workers, look around at the beginning of the year. Good places to search are in loft spaces and garden sheds, because here you may just stumble across the early stages of a queen's labours.

**The remarkable thing about a wasps' nest is that as the colony swells, the carton can be recycled, rewetted and remoulded into new shapes.**

## Fab fact

At the end of the year when the wasps' nest falls to pieces and all the workers go on strike, the big fat females – the new queens who would have now mated – need to find a spot to overwinter. It is their task to carry on through this hard time of the year, so they can start again in the spring when all other wasps have died. Look for these new queens in hiding under bark or in any cool dry place, like the potting shed. You can tell if your wasp is hibernating because it will be very still, hanging on with its jaws, and its wings will be folded down. Don't worry, she will be very sleepy, just look and then leave her be.

**You are looking for a very fragile, golf ball-shaped thing**, usually creamy white to grey in colour, suspended from the ceiling. This is the beginnings of a nest that could get to be a metre or more across in size by the end of the year!

**When a nest is at this stage, it is usually only tended by the queen.** As her first batch of daughters have not yet grown up, she starts off doing everything herself, building the first cluster of brood cells and wrapping the entire thing in a fragile envelope of 'carton' – the proper name for wasp paper. She also feeds the grubs, and incubates them once they have hatched by curling her body around the base of the cells.

**If you find one of these strange fruits**, the first thing to do is to find out whether or not the insect is in it. Many nests get abandoned at this stage because either the queen wasp decides she's made a duff decision in her nest location, or she dies or is killed. Because she has a lot on her plate, she may well be out foraging during the day. At night, however, she will return to her home, so it is at this time that you should gently approach the nest with a torch and try looking up into the nest through the entrance hole to see if she is in. If the nest is being used, sit and watch the queen at work during the day. Keep a diary of events.

**Keep an eye out and an ear open for wasps rasping away at fence posts, sheds, gates and benches. They are getting a good mandible full of wood fibre, which they combine with their saliva to make a pulp. This is then used to build their nests.**

## *Take it further*

* If the queen has abandoned her nest and you are sure she has not returned, you can collect the nest and look at it close up.

* Look for the different-coloured bands of carton on the outside, each representing a different source of wood fibre.

* Try cutting the envelope in half with scissors to show the structure inside.

# Nice pile for the wildlife

**One of the easiest ways to provide accommodation** for wildlife is to make a log pile. There's not much making involved, I know, as logs have been designed so that you just have to pile them up! Choose a good mixture of wood types and stack them, if possible, in a warm, sunny, south-facing spot.

**Why does this attract wildlife?** Well dead wood is nearly always cleared up or burnt in our very tidy and organized world, especially in the garden, but in the wild this is a very popular habitat. Not only do many creatures eat it, but it provides many damp hidey holes, too, and your log pile will do all these things and more.

**You can further improve your log pile** by doing some basic woodwork and using a drill to put holes of various sizes in the logs. These will provide shelters for small insects. You can also try making simple small boxes, like bird boxes but even smaller. Put a small round hole in one side and you will be providing a snug hide-out for anything from a homeless small mammal to a frog or toad. The bigger the pile and the more artificial burrows, the better.

**Even the tiniest of disturbances by the feet and tails** of the smallest of rodents and even invertebrates, such as beetles and millipedes, can be recorded in detail by using smoked glass or china. Provided you can protect the surface from rain and debris, this is a brilliant way of finding out exactly what is living in your log pile (see opposite).

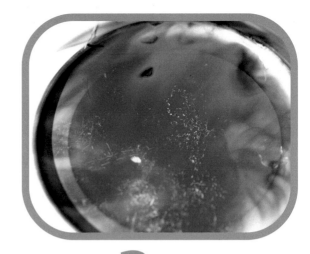

**1** Take an old plate and hold it over the flame of a candle, taking great care not to get your hands too near the flame. Keep moving the plate and don't hold it too close to the flame as china has a tendency to crack if it gets too hot. What you want is for an even layer of black carbon to be deposited on the surface.

**2** Place the plate in a sheltered place with the carbon side facing upwards. If you wish it to be used by small mammals, you can try baiting it and covering it with a makeshift shelter, such as an old roof slate balanced on stones.

**3** You will quickly get interesting tracks where animals scuff and scrape off the thin layer of carbon with their activities. It may take some imagination and interpretation to guess what creatures have made what tracks. You may also get so much activity that all you see is a jumble of traces that make no sense. Play, experiment and adapt and, with luck, you will get some very beautiful works of art.

## Take it further

If you get something you wish to keep, spray with hair spray or fixative and peel off the plate. Then display it with a back light, such as in a window.

# Homes for the hairy

**Bats live a secret life more hidden away than most other wild mammals.** Because of this, most of us will have almost no idea about what bats live in in our area or even what they look like up close. OK, so they don't make it easy for themselves, being small, active after dark and fast flying. As a result, few of us get a chance to experience the battiness of bats.

**But if things continue the way they are, there will not be any bats left.** They would have quietly squeaked their last high-frequency squeak with nobody listening or even noticing. One of the big problems they face is a lack of habitat. Bats traditionally roost in old trees, root holes, cavities and caves. They will also use railway tunnels and roof spaces, but sadly these are increasingly disappearing as we tidy up around us.

**Old trees and dead wood are less tolerated and fall down**; we spray our building timbers with toxic chemicals to stop them rotting (great for lengthening the life of a house but lethal to bats); and we either block up or go exploring caves and so disturb other roost sites. As a result, bat accommodation is at a premium and one of the best ways to help out your locals is to make your own roost sites – otherwise known as bat boxes (see opposite).

**Once finished, site your box as high as you can.** Asking a grown-up to go up a ladder is good, so that the box will be well out of the way of cats and other predators. A tree is best but you can put it on a building as well. If on a tree, it is a good idea to put up three of them, facing north, southeast and southwest. This gives the bats choice in different weather conditions. They also like a clear flight path, so choose a tree without too many branches obstructing the box.

A pipistrelle
bat.

## Cutting plan for your wood

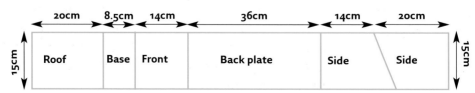

| 20cm | 8.5cm | 14cm | 36cm | 14cm | 20cm |
|------|-------|------|------|------|------|
| Roof | Base | Front | Back plate | Side | Side |

15cm     15cm

> **a plank of untreated wood that is 15cm wide, 2.5cm thick and 112.5cm long**
> **wood saw**
> **chisel**
> **3.5cm galvanised nails and wood screws**
> **hammer**
> **screwdriver**

**1** Cut up your plank according to the dimensions on the diagram. On the back plate, use the chisel to cut a groove that is 3mm deep, 2.8cm wide and 5cm from the top. Then start piecing the box together. Nail the front to the base. Then nail the sides first to the front piece ...

**2** ... and then to the back. You should have a gap of 0.5–2cm at the bottom between the base and back, which is how the bats get in and out of their box.

**3** If your wood is not rough sawn, then rough it up. Scratch the surface with a nail, especially on the inside. Think about how bats move around. They like to hang on and clamber about with their tiny clawed feet and fingers, so they need a good grippy surface if they are to move around inside your box.

**4** Screw down the lid so that nothing will disturb your bats. But if you ever need to clean out the box, you can remove the screws. It is against the law to disturb your bats, even if you have given them somewhere to live.

**5** It isn't easy to know for sure if you have bats. Keep an eye at a distance and you may start noticing a stain by the entrance. Of course, if you watch carefully on a summer evening, you may see your bats flitting around. Whatever you do, resist the temptation to take a peak.

# Make a hedgehog happy

**Hedgehogs are a fine garden inhabitant** not only because they are interesting little mammals that can be encouraged relatively easily into your home patch, but also because of their liking for garden enemy number one – the slug and, of course, its crunchier relative, the snail.

**So how do you attract hedgehogs?** Well you should be getting the hang of this by now as it's the basic principle to attracting any animal: provide shelter and food.

**Feeding hedgehogs** has traditionally been a case of putting out a bowl of milk and bread. But this mixture is too rich for them and you could be giving them more than just indigestion; you could kill them instead. So it is best to provide a hedgehog either with cat or dog food or even some of the commercially available hedgehog food in a shallow bowl along with another one of water.

**Because hedgehogs will overcome almost all obstacles** to get at some good grub, you can get them used to outdoor lights very easily, and slowly you could train your hogs to come closer to the house by simply moving the food bowls a metre or so at a time closer to the house.

**How do you know you have a hog?** Well, the most common evidence that they have passed in the night is, literally, what they've passed in the night! Hedgehog droppings are often found on lawns and they are usually small, shiny black and cylindrical, about 3–4cm long and about 1cm wide.

**In the United States, a small mammal such as an opossum, gopher, shrew or rabbit might be attracted to a home like this one.**

> **a quiet corner**
> **large board for propping against a wall**
> **a collection of dead leaves, grass and straw**

**2** Then collect some dead leaves and grass and perhaps a little straw.

**3** Stuff the cavity behind the board with your leaves, grass and straw to make it as cosy as possible. Then sit back and wait.

**1** To make your garden hedgehog friendly can be done right now, it's that easy. You could simply lean a board against a shed in a quiet, sheltered spot.

### Take it further

In the summer, put a nest box in a quiet place in your garden. Half-fill it with leaves and disguise it with some branches. Keep watch to see if a hedgehog or other similar sized mammal is attracted.

# Mammal observation box

**If you live somewhere where there doesn't appear to be any hedgehogs,** then what about those small rodents? And before you get all squeamish about rats and mice and all the horrible things they are supposed to do, just remember that these creatures have managed to survive alongside us and exploit our own untidy habits. So they deserve a little bit more thought than most people would tend to give them.

**But as well as species that your local exterminator** will try to convince you are vermin, you can also attract many other 'nice' and truly wild and native species of rodent such as voles, squirrels and shrews. All you need to do is adapt the principle of a bird table – I call it a mammal box – and here is how to make one. This works best if you have French-style or patio doors.

**Voles are one of several common species of small mammal that can be attracted to your observation box.**

## Cutting plan for your wood

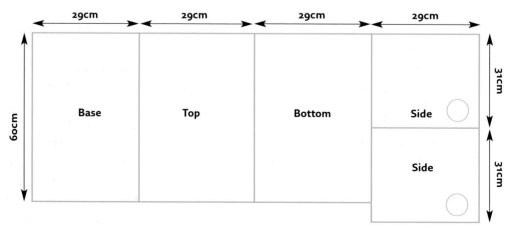

60cm

| 29cm | 29cm | 29cm | 29cm |

Base

Top

Bottom

Side

31cm

Side

31cm

## YOU WILL NEED

> 116 x 62 x 1cm piece of plywood
> saw
> electric drill with plug cutter and wood drill bit
> 2.5cm galvanized wood screws
> Phillips screwdriver
> two 30cm pieces plastic pipe with 5cm diameter
> desk lamp
> red light bulb

**1** Ask an adult to help you cut out the pieces of wood, following the diagram opposite. Drill some drainage holes on the bottom. Also cut holes for where you want your plastic pipes to enter the box.

**2** Screw together the pieces in the following order:
* Screw sides to base with holes towards the bottom.
* Screw back to base and sides.
* Screw top to base and sides (as photographed).
You then have a box with a top, bottom, two sides and a back, but no front.

**3** Take the plastic pipes and scratch the insides with an old nail or, if you can't do this, run a piece of rope or string on the inside. Both of these ideas will encourage the mammals to climb up the pipes. Push the plastic pipes into the holes on the sides.

**4** Then all you need do is position your mammal observation box up against a window, bait and wait. Once a mammal appears, try looking at it with a desk lamp containing a red light bulb. The bulb shouldn't startle your visitor and slowly you can bring it closer to the box and enjoy what you see.

# Who's living at the end of your garden?

**Once you are settled down in front of the telly** in the evening, watching your favourite soap, you would be surprised at what creatures come out of hiding within your neighbourhood. Even deep in the city, eyes are opening and whiskers are twitching as the night shift wakes up and goes about its business. But without staying up and mounting an all-night vigil, how do you get to know what's been going on? Well, here are a few tricks and techniques to help you piece together the secret activities of your surprising neighbours.

**You may find the odd dropping on your lawn** or at the base of your garden hedge, but if you simply wrinkle your nose and ignore it, you will be passing up a real treasure trove of information. Now, you may not get that excited by the prospect of dung, but for many mammals this is often the closest you can get. Without going into identification of droppings in great detail (this is a job for another book), you can tell an awful lot if you look at them through the right eyes. Ask yourselves the following questions: How big is it? What's it made of? What is its shape and where is it?

**When looking at the size,** its width will immediately give you a clue to the size of the animal's bottom, which, odd though this may seem, in most cases is related to the overall size of the animal!

**Then have a close squint to see what it's made of,** but be careful not to get your face too close. Use a stick or something to break the dropping apart and you may get a clue as to what the animal has been eating. Look out for traces of bone, fur, plant seeds and fibres and the hard bits of insects, as these obviously tell you what was for dinner but also who was doing the eating. For example, a twisted dropping with fur and bones was made by a wild carnivore while a fibrous pellet was produced by a herbivorous mammal.

**The tubular, twisted shape of this dropping, as well as evidence of fur and bone in the dropping, say that a fox has passed through the garden.**

**Some droppings are very distinctive in their design.** Rabbits and deer produce pellets that are dropped randomly, while badgers in Europe leave their droppings in little pits. Foxes like placing theirs in high-up and obvious places, like on top of stones or at the edges of paths.

**If you have a suspicious hole in a hedge,** or an obvious 'run' (which looks like a path through long grass) that crosses your garden, there are a few ways you can work out who uses them.

Prints of some common garden visitors: fox and dog can be hard to tell apart.

## Take it further

* We all know that soft ground like sand or mud is best for preserving footprints, so even if your garden is a little short of damp areas, you can make your own by making a 'tracking bed'. You need a tray and fine damp sand or mud (mixed up from soil and water, clay is even better).

* Simply put your soft stuff in the tray and put this on or along the animal's 'run'. The best position is somewhere where the animal cannot bypass the tracking bed and walk around it. So right next to the hole in the hedge is ideal.

* Experiment with bait such as a dish of dog food, too. In fact, use your imagination in any way you can to try to get the mysterious creature to put its foot in it!

Unless you are really lucky, the only cat print you are likely to find is of the domesticated variety. But it's worth noting so you can tell others apart.

This big teddy bear-like print, with its broad pad is the distinctive foot mark of a badger.

# Bugs and creepy crawlies

Those small creatures that the rest of the world likes to refer to as creepy crawlies are almost universally unloved at worst, or at best simply ignored. As humans we see the whole world from around the same height as our head! So things we look up to impress us, and little things we look down at tend not to. The creepy crawlies suffer twice because on top of their small size many are often totally misunderstood. This is partly due to the fact that we don't know what they actually are and also because some of them make us feel afraid, even if they are totally harmless.

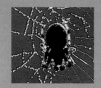

**Dare yourself to look at a spider or an ant** through a magnifying glass and you will be surprised at what you see. Even if it doesn't change how you feel about these animals and they still send you running off screaming, at least you will be more aware of what makes them what they are. You will at least be aware that they are more than just a dot with legs!

**The other thing I like about insects** and other invertebrates in that they are small; I know I may be stating the obvious here, but when you are small you do not need a lot of space. Nor do you need a lot of food. So it doesn't matter how small or desolate your space is, you will always find insect life. This is one of the reasons they are some of the most successful creatures on Earth.

**They are also cheap to attract and study.** Simply by leaving out a bit of old carpet, a small tub of water or planting a nectar-producing flowering plant in a corner, you will be creating a home for something or other!

The big, fat
female orb
spider is a
common sight in
the autumn,
sitting plumb in
the middle of a
classic spider's
web.

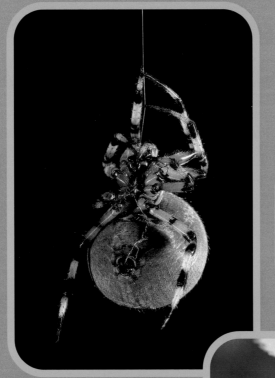

Every home – even those at the top
of tower blocks – will have ants
patrolling the walls or pavements.

These popular beetles may add a
splash of colour to the garden, but
the reds and oranges are more than
just pretty colours. They tell of
poisons and toxins, which make
ladybirds inedible to many birds and
other creatures.

They might be much feared beasts,
but earwigs cannot hurt you. They
may nibble your mum's
chrysanthemums, but the pincers
that make them easily recognizable
are used only for fighting and
folding up their wings.

# Butterfly baiting

**I guess it's similar to feeding the birds,** but providing a menu for any wildlife is one of the first steps to getting them to call in, and feeding butterflies and other insects is no exception. The way to a butterfly's loyalty is via its proboscis, and by this I mean you have to give them nectar-rich flowers for the adults to feed on. Alternatively, you can put out sweet food for them to feast on (see pages 48-9).

**Get out into the surrounding wild spaces** and look at what butterflies and other insects are attracted to and what species of flowers thrive in the soil around your area. Usually there are favourites that produce copious quantities of the sweet stuff – such as brambles, mints and other herbs – and these always seem to have a good host of winged things buzzing around them.

**Many flowers can also be a good butterfly magnet.** Take the buddleia, for example, whose purple blooms are so attractive to many species of insect, especially butterflies. In fact, so popular is it, that it has been given the common name of 'butterfly bush'.

The buddleia and the peacock butterfly go together like sharks and teeth. Just plant your bush, wait for it to flower and watch the insects come flocking in. By putting your bush in a sunny spot, you make it even more irresistible to the butterflies and bees.

> **buddleia plant**
> **glass**
> **sun**

**2** Pop the shoot in water on a window sill or just stick it straight in the ground.

**3** Very quickly it will grow roots and start sprouting.

**1** If buying a buddleia is more than your purse strings can handle, take cuttings. This is a quick and simple way to grow plants without having to sow seeds, and buddleia is easier than most other plants. Peel away a shoot from the main plant close to where it is attached. It should come away with a 'foot' on it. Remove any leaves that are near it.

## *Take it further*

\* The adult insect is only a quarter of its life cycle, so once you have lured the adults and they are happily flitting about in your bushes and borders, the next step is to make them stay. To do this you need to provide food and conditions that the often fussier egg, caterpillar and chrysalis stage require.

\* For the more common species, this can be as simple as providing a wild area of long grass. A patch of stinging nettles in a sunny place will attract the brightly coloured red admirals, commas, peacocks and small tortoiseshells, while a clump of hedge mustard and honesty and various wild members of the cabbage family will bring in the 'whites'.

\* Do your research, make your observations and plant accordingly. You will make a lot of caterpillars and other insects very happy. Once you have happy insects, you will have the beginnings of a happy habitat for all manner of other species.

# Butterfly bar

**In the late summer, many of the adult butterflies**, especially the nettle-feeding ones, such as red admiral and peacock, are loitering around getting ready for hibernation. They are cruising for sugar that they can stock up on and turn into fat, which in turn will be their survival batteries that will see them through the six months or so until the spring.

**In the garden, these butterflies are often attracted to rotten fruit.** I have a sloe bush near me which is in a sunny hot spot. The fruit ferments on the branches and the local comma butterflies can be found feeding here almost until the first frosts of winter. Other favourite feeding places are on windfall apples and plums. But if you don't have any of these natural sources of fruit, you can attract the insects with your own 'butterfly bar'.

**Once your have your bar up and running**, sit and watch to see who comes to visit. In addition to the butterflies, you may also get a few late season wasps, so it is probably best to put your bar as far away from other people and houses as possible. But at the same time, do not turn down the opportunity to see these, some of my favourite and least understood insects, up close (see also pages 32–3).

**You have created a butterfly bar. It's rather like a large version of a flower – lots of colour and a sweet, sugary reward in the middle!**

> **old soft fruit – see Step 1**
> **mixing bowl**
> **potato masher**
> **soft brown sugar**
> **old plate**

**2** Mash up the fruit in a bowl and, if necessary, add a little water to make it nice and runny. Then add some brown sugar.

**3** Dish up your fine mixture on a plate or two and leave out in the garden to attract all those hungry butterflies.

**1** Just collect some old soft fruit – maybe your local green grocer has some spoilt stock he can let you have. Bananas, apples, grapes, plums and pears are all good.

**Small comma and tortoiseshell butterflies are two species that are on the wing late into the summer and will then hibernate as adult butterflies. Because of this, they need sugar to build up their body fat reserves to see them through the cold months.**

# The shape shifters

**We tend to take the life cycles of some of our garden insects** a little bit for granted. That of the butterflies and moths is no exception; just think about it for a moment and look at the sequence of pictures opposite.

**But this miracle is by no means exclusive** and can be readily seen within the confines of a slightly modified box, bottle or empty fish tank. You can even buy a butterfly kit by mail order and see for yourself a caterpillar changing to a chrysalis and then to a butterfly.

**You can rear many different species of caterpillar** (see opposite) as long as you either see for yourself what food plant they are eating or are able to identify the type of caterpillar. Keep a record of the caterpillars and the adult moth or butterfly. A digital camera makes this very easy.

## Fab facts

* If you are really lucky, you will be able to catch the emergence of a butterfly or moth from its chrysalis. This often happens in the dark, early in the morning, as in the wild they would be very vulnerable at this time and in this way they can avoid any predators.

* Some of the big hawk moths and silk moths put on around 27,000 times their original hatching weight!

* Caterpillars shed their skins up to five times in their short lives.

**3** Supply them with branched twigs for the day they settle down to change. When they reach a certain size, caterpillars moult and underneath is no caterpillar but an odd-shaped bag, called a pupa or chrysalis. Do not disturb the chrysalides.

**1** The butterfly's cycle begins as an egg, a speck of life out of which hatches a little soft, squishy, worm-like creature. This is a caterpillar and it's born with an enormous appetite. Collect your own from among chomped leaves in the garden: cabbages, nasturtiums and young fresh nettles in sunny locations are the best places to look for the caterpillars.

**2** Put your caterpillars in your chosen container lined with a piece of kitchen paper – and always add a lid with air holes pierced in it. Feed them plenty of fresh food. This should ideally be the same plant type as you found them on, as many caterpillars are fussy eaters and will rather starve to death than eat the wrong food. Thoroughly clean the container every few days.

**4** After about ten days they will start to change colour, which means they are about to split and turn into a magnificent and beautifully coloured butterfly or moth.

# Little leaf lovers

**In summer** you may notice that some of the leaves on the trees and bushes in your park or garden have developed a strange wiggly pattern on them. Well, look closely and you will see that this pattern is not actually on the leaves but in them.

**These feats of micro-engineering are the tunnels of leaf miners,** a tiny micro moth, the adult of which is probably one of the least noticeable and unassuming creatures in your garden. It makes sense, if you are small enough to fit between the two surfaces of a leaf, that this would be a fairly safe haven from most predators.

**Backlight the tunnels of a leaf miner with a bright torch and you can see their work and sometimes even the insect inside.**

**The same principle works if you tape the leaf to a window. Look at how the tunnel starts off narrow and, as the caterpillar gets bigger and fatter, so does its tunnel.**

**YOU WILL NEED**

> **leaves with leaf miners**
> **torch**
> **magnifying glass**

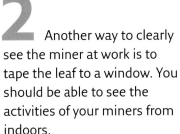

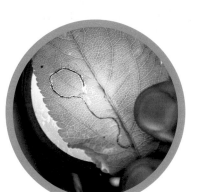

**2** Another way to clearly see the miner at work is to tape the leaf to a window. You should be able to see the activities of your miners from indoors.

**3** Look through the magnifying glass from your handy stuff (see pages 6–7) and you will see all sorts of details not noticed by the naked eye.

**1** Place a small torch behind your leaf and search the tunnels for the miner itself. You will probably see lots of droppings, but follow the tunnel to its end and here you will be able to see the silhouette of a small caterpillar. If it isn't moving, the chances are it has turned into a pupae and is waiting to hatch. If this is the case, collect the leaf and keep it in a small airtight plastic box and watch and wait to see what comes out.

## Take it further

* Place a branch of leaves containing miners in a jug of water on your window sill and keep a record of their progress – but first promise your parents that you will clean the windows once your experiment is over! Using a China marker pen, mark and plot each day's activity. Notice how the tunnel gets wider as the caterpillar inside grows fatter.

* When your miner has left the leaf, keep your mine by pressing the leaf on kitchen paper within the pages of a big book.

* There are many kinds of leaf miner. See how many you can find. Are they loyal to certain species of tree? Do different species make different-shaped mines?

# Suckers for the sweet stuff

**Now, if you think butterflies have a secret life** then you will find their nocturnal cousins, the moths, positively mysterious. During the daylight hours, they tend not to draw attention to themselves by keeping a very low profile. This is further helped by the fact that they are very well camouflaged. But when we are at our least active, they are at their most active.

**If you want to learn about the moths you have living around you,** there is a rather fun and sticky way to get to know some of them. It relies on the fact that many moths fuel their activities in the same way as butterflies by feeding on sweet, sugary liquid. This can be nectar from flowers, but just as easily it can be sap oozing from wounded plant stems, or even rotten and fermenting fruit. It seems the sweeter it is, the more they love it.

**You can cash in on this behaviour** by serving up your own sweet and sticky meal that is all pudding and no first course. It is a technique that lepidopterists (that's the name for someone who studies butterflies and moths) have been using for hundreds of years and is called 'sugaring'.

Some moths, such as one known as the 'old lady', seem to come only to sugar laid out this way. I have seen hundreds come to sugared baits while none turned up in any of the moth traps I was also running in the same garden!

## Fab fact

When you do see your moths, spend a little time watching how they are feeding. See how their eyes glow in an eerie way as they reflect your torch light back at you.

**3** At dusk, hang your sock in a tree, from the washing line, over the garden fence – or anywhere else you choose. Then leave for a few hours and return after dark with a torch to see who has turned up.

**2** When you are happy with your culinary creation, you now need to start thinking about how to serve it up. You can make 'moth socks' or you can use rope. If you are using a sock, tie a piece of string around the top and then put the sock (or rope, if using) into the mixture before it cools down. Stir it around.

**1** Put all the sweet ingredients in the saucepan and slowly heat until everything has dissolved. Add a little of the wine or rum. This helps give your mixture a great fermenting smell that will waft far and wide and tantalize the antennae of moths for miles around!

**4** Alternatively, make your mixture a little stickier by adding more sugar at the mixing stage. Paint it onto trees and fence posts in and around the garden and then, as for Step 3, come back when it's dark with your torch to see what visitors you have encouraged.

# Beguiled by bulbs

**Moths are famous for being attracted to bright lights.** The old saying, 'Like moths around a flame' not only applies to candles and fire, moths also find the modern equivalent just as mesmerizing.

**When I was a budding young naturalist** I had very little pocket money to play with – even my paper round if I did it for a year wouldn't cover the cost of a good professional moth trap. So I came up with my own solution – changing my bedroom into a giant moth trap.

**Stay up after dark and turn on all the lights in your bedroom** and keep the curtain or blinds open. After an hour or two you will start to see various moths turning up on your window and even the occasional large beetle will come whirring by, bouncing noisily off the panes of glass.

**Some of the moths will settle and stay still,** which will allow you to see them up close and inspect them through the window with a magnifying glass. The only problem is that seeing their top side is the best way of actually identifying them and to do this you have to open the window and let them in. But do this and you will run the risk of making yourself very unpopular with your family – especially when you let in all the neighbourhood mosquitoes and midges too.

## Fab fact

Why do so many nocturnal insects get drawn to light? Well there has to be a reason, but why this common behaviour occurs is one of those real mysteries of nature. One of the best theories is that moths use natural light such as the moon and the stars to navigate in a straight line. Because these lights are far away, this works, but when the lights are closer to them – our artificial electric moons and stars – these become a bit of a distraction and cause them to fly in ever decreasing circles until they are head butting the bulb!

The lephant hawk moth is one of the largest moths you are likely to see.

The magpie moth is one of the prettiest.

## Take it further

* If you find that you seriously start getting into moths, there are a few cheaper types of proper moth traps available and this would make a pretty fantastic birthday or Christmas present.

* The trap featured here is a basic, affordable and portable trap of the 'Heath type' design. It is perfect for beginners and the way it works is very straightforward. The tube light attracts the moth, which then falls down into the collection box full of egg cartons.

* If you get really serious, you may decide it is time to spend much more money on a very posh one.

# Plant bugs

**What is an aphid?** Well, these tiny little sap-sucking insects may be well known to gardeners who continually wage war against them as they mount their annual attack on rose bushes and other plants every summer. But to the rest of us?

**That sticky stuff that covers your car windscreen** if you park under the wrong species of tree in the summer is honey dew. This is a pleasant phrase for the excrement that is produced by aphids. To find out a bit more about what honey dew is, how it is used and produced, there is a little demonstration you can do (see opposite).

**Once caught, look through a magnifying glass** at the head end of the aphid and you will notice the straw-like mouth parts that it stabs into plant stems and uses to tap the neverending flow of sap. As the liquid passes through its body, the aphid takes what it needs and the rest drops onto the leaf and creates a habitat for moulds. Ants may feed on it, too, and sometimes it is so plentiful that it drops out of the tree and gets stuck on the windscreen of any car parked beneath.

## Fab fact

In two months, a single aphid can, in theory, give rise to six million new aphids! With figures like this if they were all to survive, there would be no point gardening. But fortunately many creatures rely on them as food, including wasps, ladybirds, lacewings and many bird populations.

**1** Either find a sacrificial pot plant that already has a population of greenfly or black fly, or forage around in the garden for an unfortunate plant that is being sucked dry. Cut yourself a branch or stem and put this in water.

**2** To stop infecting every other plant in the house – something that plant-loving mums and dads would not be too happy about – remove all the insects with wings with a pair of tweezers or a cocktail stick into a bowl and take outside. Now you are ready to observe the secrets of your herds in the herbaceous border.

**3** Scrutinize the colony through a magnifying glass and you will notice insects of varying sizes. The biggest ones will be the adult females. These will be reproducing at an incredible rate as they do not need a male to mate with. They are simply baby factories and they produce clones of themselves, churning out up to ten a day. Inside these babies there will already be more babies developing!

## Take it further

* Although these bugs look completely defenceless, they do have a number of escape tactics. The first can be seen if you tickle a colony with a paintbrush. A lot of them simply let go of the twig or bud on which they are feeding.

* Some will also present their rear end to an attacker and ooze a waxy substance out of the two prongs on either side of their abdomen. Called siphunculi (or honey dew), this is sticky and unpleasant, especially as it solidifies on the mouth parts or the eyes of a ladybird. If you watch a ladybird going about its business, it often has to stop to clean itself of this gunk.

# The 'wig' trap

**Many insects are thigmatropic,** which means they 'love to squeeze their bodies into impossibly tight spaces'. They do this as a safety measure because tight spaces are hard to access for most predators. Also, if you are a small invertebrate, the chances are the shelter provided helps prevent the loss of moisture through exposure.

**Among their number are creatures** such as the instantly recognizable earwig. If you look at one from the side, you will see it looks rather flattened, which means it can jam itself into small gaps. Other creatures that have similar habits are cockroaches and woodlice. The enterprising naturalist can make the most of this behaviour by making an earwig trap.

**There are several good designs,** but one of the best is that used by some growers of prize show flowers, who are not too keen on earwigs, because of their habit of sitting in chrysanthemum flowers and having a nibble. The steps opposite show you how to make one in the same way.

**Tell Mr and Mrs Wig apart: this one is a male as he has a much larger set of pincers on the end of his abdomen.**

**1** Take the flower pot and stand your stick up in the centre. Then stuff the straw or grass around the stick.

**2** Dribble lots of honey onto the straw and then, very carefully, so that you don't spill the honey onto your clothes ...

**3** ... turn the earwig trap upside down and push the stick into the ground at your chosen spot. A good place is somewhere that is lightly shaded.

**4** The next day, come back with a plastic container and investigate the contents of your trap to see what you've caught.

## Take it further

* Variations on this earwig trap are made by using old rags or bits of carpet screwed up and draped over branches.

* Or make up rolls of corrugated cardboard and leave in similar dark places.

# Rulers of the patio

**The patio is where it all started for me.** Getting down on my hands and knees and watching the frantic wars and struggles of the ants, their efficient foraging and fascinating dramas all acted out at a tiny scale right in front of my nose, was quite amazing. The little insights I gained from this Lilliputian world made me look at nature through completely different eyes. Follow the experiments below and opposite and you, too, will soon learn a lot about ants.

## Nick's trick

Try to persuade an ant returning to the nest to walk over the glass or perspex. As soon as it has obliged, sprinkle some talcum powder on the glass and blow off the excess. What you will just be able to see is a faint line of talc where it has stuck to the liquid the ant has oozed out of its bottom. This is a neat trick, but it doesn't work well with all species and some ants will leave better and juicier trails. Give it a go.

## Fab fact

An ant has two tiny stomachs. The contents of the second one is shared with the rest of the colony – a kind of community stomach!

**1** On a hot sunny day cut a square piece from a black bin bag and stick it to the patio with gaffer tape. Put a small dollop of honey or jam in the middle of it. Watch and wait. There will be ants walking in a random 'drunken' way all over the patio, but eventually one will stumble upon the paradise you have created and it will quickly stuff its little face with a sample and run as fast and as straight as it can back to the nest.

**2** What you can't see is that the ant is dragging its bottom, leaving a trail of perfume. This is produced by a special organ known as the dufours gland. When an ant returns to the nest it shares samples of its find with its nest mates, who then set off back along the scent trail to the bait.

**3** Soon you will notice the numbers start to increase around the food. Each ant returning to the nest does the same thing, and the numbers being recruited to the bait just keep swelling. In this way, the tiny ants can use the strength of their numbers to exploit any food they find. As the food runs out, the ants will return to the nest without food and the excitement starts to wane. The scent trail is not reinforced and it eventually dries up and evaporates.

### Take it further

* You can have some fun with your ants to demonstrate the total reliance on the scent trail. Watch the path the ants are travelling along and when you have a gap, quickly smudge the trail with your finger, wiping it backwards and forwards.

* Watch what happens – when they come to the gap, the ants panic! They scatter and lose their organization. Eventually, in the frantic quest for the trail, one will find it and order will be restored.

# Handy stuff: bottle trap

**Plastic drinks bottles are horrible.** Tricky to recycle and around for ever, what should we do with them? Well one way to recycle them is to use them to make a 'pitfall trap', which is just one lazy way to find out what smaller creatures are roaming around in the nettle patch, on the lawn or in the rockery – especially at night. Follow the steps opposite and then come back the next day to discover what you've caught.

Turn out the contents of your trap into a tub to sort out your catch and to observe the kinds of creatures that were crawling about in your garden, most usually after dark.

Here we have caught a couple of species of ground beetle. These animals are active hunters, running around in the garden eating other insects, and some species even specialize in slug munching. So when you have finished studying them, release your catch and you can let them get on with garden pest control.

**2** Put the rotten fruit in the bottom of the main body of the bottle. Smelly meat will attract carnivorous beetles, or dead leaves will attract other types of animal or insect.

**3** Invert the top part of the bottle inside the main body.

**1** Take your drinks bottle and cut around it about 10cm from the neck. You are left with a 'pit' and a funnel. Remove the lid from the funnel.

**4** Choose your spot and dig a hole that is the same size and depth as the body of the bottle. Put the bottle in it so that the rim is level with the surface of the soil and then replace the loose soil around the bottle.

**5** Place the flat stone, old tile or board over the top so that any passing animals can get underneath but any rain will not fill up the trap, killing any animals that get caught.

# Worm world

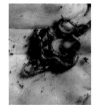

**Most of the time we pay them no attention.** They are the pink wiggly things that usually make kids go 'yuk!' or adults moan about because they make a mess of the lawn. But there is much more to worms than meets the eye. Not only are they vital to the health of soil, but they are good food for many creatures we love, such as badgers, hedgehogs and many birds. Worms are also fascinating animals.

**You may find them drowning in puddles on pavements on rainy days** or uncovered when you are digging. But to see a worm at its best you need to get out after dark and do a little bit of worm watching. Take a torch with you and cover it with a thin layer of transparent red cellophane so that you produce a red light the worms will not be sensitive to. Yes – they can see. Worms may not be able to form images like we do, but they are sensitive to light. Shine a torch on one without the red covering and you will see what I mean.

**The best nights to go worm watching** are the warm, wet ones. Walk carefully and slowly around on the grass and you could get to see worms with their front parts out of their burrows. If you are really lucky, you may see worms grabbing dead leaves with their mouths and pulling them back into their burrows to eat.

**Next time you find a worm, give it a few seconds of your time.** Get to know it a bit better. They don't have ears, but they are nonetheless very sensitive to vibration. Supposing you were to talk to it, which end would you strike up conversation with? Which end is the worm's head? Well, put you worm down and it will be easy enough to work out. The worm's pointed end is where the mouth is and the blunt and flattened tip is the rear of the worm.

## Nick's trick

It looks ridiculous, but it is a lot of fun; it's called puddling or worm charming. Gulls do this on wet playing fields. You stamp up and down on the spot while pouring water on the ground at the same time. After a few minutes of this activity, worms should start to come to the surface.

**You can tell if your worm is fully grown. If it has a saddle (or clittelum) – a broad band across its middle – you can be sure it's an adult as young worms do not have one of these.**

## Take it further

* One of the things that is cool about worms is the way they move through the soil. Let one wiggle about on your palm until it finds its way between your fingers – feel how strong it is!

* Feel the motion of the worm – the way it stretches out and becomes thin so it can squeeze between your fingers. It then contracts, squishing the watery body fluids up to the front end, forcing your fingers apart. That is exactly how it moves through the soil.

* To help it grip the tunnel walls, worms also have very strong bristles along their bodies. These are known as setae and you can feel them if you gently pull a worm backwards between your fingers. They feel rough, which is quite surprising for a creature that looks so wet and soft! These setae are also the reason blackbirds have such a hard job pulling worms out of their tunnels on the lawn.

# Webbed wonder

**It sometimes seems a shame to think that those gorgeous orb webs** that you find draped in the shrubbery or hanging in the hedgerow rarely last longer than a day. Being fragile is, of course, part of their attraction, and from the spider's point of view they are designed as disposable and recyclable insect traps. However, it is possible to preserve these structures and even hang them on your own wall.

**First of all, choose a nice still day and find a real beauty of a web.** Make sure it is dry (no droplets of dew) and make sure its maker, the spider, isn't in residence (check well in and around the edges of the web, especially in curled-up leaves) as it really won't appreciate what comes next! Then follow the steps opposite to make your own lovely spider's web picture.

## Fab facts

* Spiders can be found out at sea and in the air, even as high as 3,000 metres. They form part of a strange world of aerial plankton that drift around on air currents. Spiders don't have wings, so how on earth do they get up there?

* Some of them do it by 'ballooning'. Go out on a dewy autumn morning and just about any long grass will be laced with dew-laden strands of silk.

* Investigate closely and you may find lots of tiny 'money' spiders. If you collect one on the tip of a finger and hold it up to the breeze or blow on it, you may persuade it to 'balloon' for you.

* The spider will raise itself up and the breeze will pull out a thread of silk, which will snake up on the wind. When this develops enough lift to overcome the weight of the spider, it lets go and goes drifting.

YOU WILL NEED

> spray paint, white or black is a good choice
> newspaper or large sheet of paper
> artist's fixative (available from art and crafts shops) or hair spray
> a piece of card large enough for your web to fit onto and contrasting in colour to your choice of spray paint
> scissors

**1** Take the can of spray paint and, holding a sheet of newspaper behind the web to stop you getting paint all over the plants, spray the web evenly and lightly on both sides from a distance of about 40cm. Get too close and you will blow a hole in your web. Leave it to dry for a while and repeat.

**2** Spray artist's fixative or hair spray onto the web to make it super-sticky. Repeat on the other side, just as you did with the spray paint.

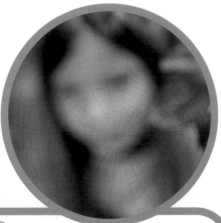

**3** Before the glue dries, take the card and line it up perfectly with the web. Slowly and carefully push the card onto the silk so it sticks in the right place first time. Once the web has touched the card you cannot change your mind without ending up in a messy tangle! Use scissors to cut the supporting strands and give the web and card another coat of fixative to make sure it's securely held in place.

## Take it further

Once you've finished your web, mount this spider's original in a frame and hang it on your wall. You could measure all the strands of silk and work out how much silk was needed to make your web, and even collect the webs made by different species of spider.

# Going further

This book was never meant to be anything but the very beginning of a journey – I see it as being the map, the compass and a kick in the right direction. As you continue to explore your garden and park, you will begin to ask more questions and discover things that this book may not be able to answer. This is why this section exists – to give you a few more pointers in the right direction.

## Good reading

*Birdfeeder Handbook* by Robert Burton (Dorling Kindersley). **It's not all about nuts and this book shows you why. A great book on the art of turning your garden into a bird reserve.**

*The BTO Nest Box Guide* by Chris du Feu. **This is a classic book on the art of building nest boxes; from common to specialised and with plenty of variations on a theme. If you are serious about your garden birds, this must be on your shelf. It is also quiet cheap.**

*Chris Packham's Back Garden Nature Reserve* (New Holland). **A very readable and entertaining guide to the residents of an average garden; how to deal with them, enjoy them and encourage them.**

*Garden Creepy Crawlies* by Michael Chinery (Whittet Books). **My favourite book as far as explaining the lives of our common garden inverts without being patronising or dull. A great value book worth every penny of pocket money.**

*Identifying Birds by Behaviour* by Dominic Couzens (Collins). **Very good companion to a basic field guide, it gives you a good idea of how to get to know birds by their general impression, size and shape (GISS). It also introduces the idea of actually watching your birds and what they do rather than just identifying and ticking and then moving on.**

*Illustrated Keys* (Field Studies Council, www.field-studies-council.org). **These easy-to-use illustrated keys are fantastic and lightweight, contain lots of information and are very cheap at just a few pounds each; there is a huge range of subjects covered.**

*Naturalists Handbooks* (Richmond Publishing). **In the range are several titles that the keen garden naturalist may find indispensable, especially Ladybirds, Ants and Animals under Logs and Stones.**

*The Wildlife-friendly Garden'* by Michael Chinery (Collins), *The Bird-friendly Garden'* by Stephen Moss (Collins) and *The First-time Naturalist* by Nick Baker (Collins) **are three more general books that provide you with a good background.**

## Handy organizations

**The Mammal Society:** A charity focused on conserving and studying our fluffy fauna. They have many great publications as well as a website giving you information about up-coming surveys that you can get involved with and there's also a great 'fun stuff' section too – www.abdn.ac.uk/mammal/ or telephone 020 7350 2200.

**Royal Society for the Protection of Birds (RSPB):** They really are the big ones; not only an organization that gives the birds a lot but also the members. Numbers speak for themselves as the RSPB has over a million members. Great magazines too – for adults and kids. They produce many handy leaflets with information pertaining specifically to the garden too – www.rspb.org.uk or telephone 01767 680551.

**The Wildlife Trusts:** They are a countrywide organization and there will be a regional group near you organizing lots of 'wildlifing' activities for all ages. The Wildlife Trust also produce regular magazines for both grown-ups and younger members and they have a junior wing called Wildlife watch. This is an organization I would love to have joined when I was a kid but didn't know about, so that's why I'm telling you now – www.wildlifetrusts.org or telephone 0870 0367711.

# Handy stuff - equipment supplies and other contacts

*Anglian Lepidopterists supplies:* I went looking for the cheapest and best moth traps and I found them here; lots of options for those young entomologists who are on a budget (just remember how much a Playstation costs when looking at the web site!). Also stocks of the bigger, more expensive toys too; very helpful and friendly – www.angleps.btinternet.co.uk or telephone 01263 862068.

*CJ Wildbird Foods:* Produce an annual handbook of garden feeding and wildlife care; it's another one-stop shop for feeds, seeds and cover for your garden fauna, lots of advice too – www.birdfood.co.uk or telephone 0800 731 2820.

*Eco-watch:* Mission impossible on a bird seed budget, this company specialises in wildlife surveillance and they have the toys to prove it – www.eco-watch.com or telephone 01726 843744.

*Ernest and Charles:* One of the big suppliers of garden wildlife products in the UK; from bird seed to books, bird boxes to hedgehog homes they have it all – www.ernest-charles.com or telephone 08007316770.

*Interplay UK Ltd:* Makers and suppliers of fine educational, science-based toys. If you are having trouble with your ants, Interplay produce a great 'world of ants' and also a 'wormery' especially for younger naturalists – www.interplay.co.uk or telephone 01628 488944.

# Index

# Author's acknowledgements

> Big thanks to the energetic and hard-working team at Harper Collins who put this book together. Especially the tireless Helen Brocklehurst - how she holds everything together when it comes to building books, I don't know. But thankfully she does and she's good at it. And the same for Emma Callery, who as editor for this book has endured the frustrating half-finished manuscripts, bad grammar and spelling and, of course, the continual frustration of not being able to get hold of me on the phone! Thanks for not shouting at me and getting cross! Nikki English, the photographer, who has the patience of a saint and found the energy to continue wrangling animals and children both at the same time AND managing to take great photographs; surely the definition of multi-tasking!

> Sarah Childs-Carlile for the use of her garden and the brilliant models Barney, Billie, Clare, Hattie, Hepsie, Matthew, Solly and Victoria.